365

Ways
to Live to
100

365

Ways
to Live to

100

Siimon Reynolds

Andrews McMeel
Publishing

Kansas City

∾

01 02 03 04 05 BIN 10 9 8 7 6 5 4 3 2 1

Library of Congress Cataloging-in-Publication Data
Reynolds, Siimon.
365 ways to live to 100 / Siimon Reynolds.
    p. cm.
Includes bibliographical references.
ISBN 0-7407-1020-6 (pbk.)
    1. Longevity—Miscellanea. 2. Aging—Miscellanea. 3.
Self-care, Health. I. Title: Three hundred sixty five ways to
live to 100. II. Title.
RA776.75 .R49 2000
613—dc21   00-061787

Book design by Holly Camerlinck

To Brian,
a true pioneer of
antiaging medicine.

Introduction

∾

Once we thought a long, healthy life was in the lap of the gods; now, however, we know that there are specific things we can do to slow down and even reverse the aging process.

I've collected the best of these methods in one short, sharp, easy-to-understand book.

365 Ways to Live to 100 is a summary of the hundreds of hours I have spent studying this subject, perusing mountains of books, attending scores of lectures, and conducting interviews with the world's top antiaging specialists.

This book also features many of the techniques we utilize at the Redwood Anti-Aging

Clinic, Australia's first and largest antiaging medical center.

Put this book into practice and not only are you likely to live longer, but the days you live will be filled with energy, vitality, and optimism.

Sound great?

Well then, let's get started . . .

365
Ways
to Live to
100

1

Stick to Heart Association Guidelines

∞

The American Heart Association recommends that your intake of dietary fat should be less than 30 percent of your total calories, and saturated fat less than 10 percent of your total fat intake.

2

Take Folic Acid Daily

∾

Up to 50,000 deaths from heart disease could
be prevented each year if Americans consumed
more folic acid. You'll find folic acid in leafy
vegetables, carrots, egg yolk, pumpkin, and beans,
as well as in supplements from your health-food
store.

3

Get a Pet

∾

Studies have shown that pet owners live longer and happier lives than do those who don't own a furry friend.

4

Exercise Daily

∽

It's the ultimate longevity technique. Vigorous
daily exercise increases the body's production of
human growth hormone, which helps regenerate
your body's cells. It also reduces stress (a crucial
factor in aging).

5

Follow Dr. David Ryback's Anticancer Diet

෬

- Eat whole-grain bread, cereal or pasta, or brown rice at least four times a day.
- Eat at least two servings a day of citrus fruits, green peppers, or tomatoes.
- Eat broccoli, cabbage, carrots, or cauliflower at least once a day.
- Enjoy beans or tea a few times a week.
- Be vegetarian or choose fish or fowl over red meat.

6

Train Your Brain

∾

Play board games, do a crossword, read a book, play an instrument, or involve yourself socially. Use your brain regularly and it can remain sharp until you're one hundred and beyond.

7

Laugh a Lot

୧୭

When we laugh, the brain produces "feel good" chemicals called endorphins, which are believed to improve our immune response.

8

Study Fire Prevention

- Don't end up a statistic.
- Install a smoke alarm in your home.
- Buy a fire blanket and a fire extinguisher.
- Don't smoke in bed.

9

Be Orderly

෨

Of twelve hundred centenarians surveyed by Dr. Walter Bortz on the secrets of long life, 90 percent nominated the role of order in their lives.

So plan your life, stick to proven systems, and keep your mind clear.

10

Listen to
Relaxation Tapes

෬

They work wonders on your stress levels. For
best results, choose subliminal tapes—they
combine soothing music with positive affirmations.

11

Keep Three
First-Aid Kits Handy

∾

Most families don't have even one first-aid kit.
But to be really safe, you need one in your
house, one in your workplace, and one in the car.

12

Breast-feed Your Baby

⁀

Recent evidence suggests that babies breast-fed for six months or more have a considerably lower risk of developing brain tumors, leukemia, or lymphoma.

13

Be an Optimist

You are what you think you are. Optimists are less stressed, simply because they believe everything will be okay.

14

The Daily Siesta

∾

A brief afternoon nap has been found to boost longevity. A recent study in Athens found that men who napped thirty minutes or more a day were 30 percent less likely to develop heart problems.

15

Aspirin Isn't Just for Headaches

෴

A five-year study of more than 22,000 men by researchers at the Brigham and Women's Hospital in Boston found that aspirin may reduce the risk of heart attack by 44 percent.

16

Limit Animal Protein

∽

Most of us eat 30 percent too much—and it can be harmful because it's often high in saturated fat and cholesterol (which can lead to clogging of the arteries).

17

Don't Cook Out
the Vitamins

❧

Oversoaking or cooking vitamin-rich foods may
reduce your intake of vitamins B and C.

For example, boiled cabbage loses 75 percent of
its vitamin C content; peas lose up to 40 percent
of their thiamine after just five minutes of cooking.

18

Take a Bath

∽

Increasing your body temperature—by exercise
or even just soaking in a hot tub—can help
induce sleep.

19

Say So Long to Salt

❦

Not only does salt lead to hardening of the arteries, but a high salt intake could also lead to blood-pressure problems.

20

Walk Off
Your Depression

∞

Studies have found that exercise is good for
more than just the body; it can improve your
mental outlook. Three to five weeks of regular
exercise is all it takes.

21

Drink Away
Your Wrinkles

∾

Dr. John Bland describes water as the best antiaging "vitamin" for your skin. Well-hydrated skin stays smoother and is less prone to wrinkling.

22

Have Sex Often

෨

Use it or lose it! Regular sex is said to be one of
the best ways of keeping your sexual organs
healthy and functioning until old age.

23

Be in the Flow

෩

Professor Mihaly Csikszentmihalyi says happiness is caused by a state he calls "flow"—a halfway point between being relaxed and being stressed.

The message: fill your life with challenging, involving activities that you do well.

24

Eat Your Onions

❦

Chinese researchers believe that consumption of
onion and garlic lowers the incidence of
stomach cancer.

25

Follow Dr. Robert Goldman's Antidepression Plan

∽

- Increase your intake of vitamins B_6 and B_{12}, folic acid, and riboflavin.
- Eliminate sugar and caffeine.
- Get thirty minutes of sunlight a day and work in well-lit rooms.
- Eat plenty of complex carbohydrates.
- Consider taking DLPA.
- Load up on foods with omega-3 fatty acids (like fish).
- Try Saint-John's-wort.
- Exercise vigorously three times a week.

26

Have a Regular Pap Test

∾

Women: cancer experts recommend that you get a Pap test every two years. The five-year survival rate for uterine cancer (which a Pap test detects) is over 85 percent if it's caught early.

27

Watch Out for the Wok

૭૦

Chinese wok cooks have the same lung cancer rate as American women—yet they smoke only half as much.

Researchers believe the wok is the culprit. So if you must use a wok, do so in a well-ventilated kitchen and keep the oil temperature down.

28

Inspect Your Body Regularly

૭๑

Cancers of the testes and breasts can be detected early by self-examination. Learn how to do it from your doctor.

29

Peel Your Fruits
and Vegetables

∽

Pesticide residues can remain on your fruit and
vegetables even after you've washed them. A
recent study found that trimming celery reduced
residues of methomyl (an insecticide believed to
cause cancer) by 50 to 90 percent.

30

Keep the Noise Down

∾

Australian studies indicate that people who listen to loud music through headphones are at risk of major hearing problems in later life.

31

Take Planes for Long Trips

ᦁ

Statistically, planes and trains are far safer than cars. So if you want to minimize your risk of a fatal accident, take a plane or train.

32

Try Deprenyl

∾

Studies with rats have shown that Deprenyl (or Eldepryl)—a drug used mainly for treating Parkinson's disease—slows the aging process while boosting sexual activity and learning ability.

The drug is available only by prescription, and should be taken in small, authorized doses.

33

Watch for Gene Medicine

∞

Is gene therapy the future of antiaging medicine?

There are reportedly well over one hundred clinical trials of gene-based therapies under way. These and others may hold the key to the development of medical procedures to destroy and replace defective genes.

34

Try Estrogen

∽

Research shows that estrogen may:

- Increase longevity
- Reduce cholesterol and heart disease
- Strengthen bones

But it should be used only under strict medical supervision.

35

Don't Smoke Dope

∽

Marijuana is more carcinogenic than tobacco
(especially as a cause of lung cancer), is harder
on the lungs, and has been linked to
schizophrenia.

36

Wear Sunglasses

∾

You won't just look cool; you may reduce your risk of developing cancer of the eye caused by exposure to the sun's ultraviolet (UV) rays.

But choose sunglasses carefully—more than 40 percent don't filter UV rays.

37

Beware of
Slimming Remedies

෨෨

Slimming products containing germander have
been linked to severe liver poisoning, while two
Oriental herbs sometimes used in dieting
products—*Stephania tetrandra* and *Magnolia
officinalis*—can lead to kidney problems.

38

Use Artificial Sweeteners Sparingly

༺༻

Many artificial sweeteners are made with cyclamates or saccharin, both of which have been linked in animal studies to bladder cancer. While there is no conclusive evidence of the effect on humans, it's better to be safe than sorry.

39

Check Electromagnetic Fields

∽

Various studies have linked exposure to electromagnetic fields to leukemia, Alzheimer's disease, and decreased immune system efficiency.

So don't live near power lines, and keep your use of electrical appliances to a minimum.

40

Wear a Seat Belt

∾

In a high-speed crash, no amount of air bags will save a driver who's not wearing a seat belt. Buckle up and your chances of living increase greatly.

41

Take Smart Drugs

෨

Nootropics, the so-called brain-enhancing drugs,
are prescribed in Germany for slight memory
disturbances and general brain boosting.

Ask your doctor about Piracetam, Deprenyl,
Clonidine, or acetyl-L-carnitine.

42

Enjoy the Magic of Sleeping Potions

∾

The root of an herb known as valerian has been found to reduce the time it takes to get to sleep. Other sleep aids include kava kava, GABA (gamma aminobutyric acid), chamomile, and lemon balm tea, as well as lavender oil in a warm bath.

43

Ask Yourself
Anthony Robbins's
Morning Power Questions

∽

- What am I excited about in life right now?
- What am I happy about in my life?
- What am I enjoying in my life right now?
- What am I grateful for in my life right now?
- Who do I love and who loves me, and how does that make me feel?

44

Don't Eat Much for Dinner

෨ᙡ

Studies show that people who eat most of their calories at breakfast and lunch lose more weight than people who eat the same amount late at night.

That's because they burn off their calories during the day. An evening meal gets digested while you're asleep.

45

Fall in Love

∽

Scientists have found that people in love are less stressed and tend to produce more age-reducing hormones (such as estrogen, progesterone, DHEA, and human growth hormone).

And because they're happier, they have a stronger immune system.

46

Seek the Best Doctor

❦

When it comes to treating cancer, different doctors have different success rates. Finding the right one can significantly increase your chances of a cure—so shop around.

47

Know Your Disease

∽

If you have a serious disease, knowledge is power. Become an expert: check relevant alternative-medicine sites on the Internet, and search out the finest books.

Stretch It

According to Dr. John Bland, the benefits of daily stretching exercises include more nutrients to the muscles, injury prevention, increased range of motion, improved body shape, reduced muscle tension and pain, and better coordination.

49

Pray

∽

Dr. Herbert Benson says that research shows that people who pray regularly have lower cholesterol levels, less stress, and significantly less risk of heart attack.

They're also happier.

50

Beat That Cold

❦

As a natural cold remedy recommended by
Taoists, try grating horseradish and mixing it with
lemon juice to form a paste; take half a teaspoon
two or three times a day.

51

Walk ... It Works

෬

A good walk is great medicine for people with lung disease, arthritis, osteoporosis, or hardening of the arteries—and best of all, you can do it into your nineties and beyond.

52

Know the Facts of Cancer

∾

Cancer is a lot more preventable than most of us think—in fact, researchers believe that 68 percent of all cancer cases could be prevented.

Much of our immunity depends on what we eat, drink, and breathe, as well as our mental state.

53

Visualize Being Young

॰৺৹

Researchers have found that your subconscious accepts any information given to it (regardless of its truth).

So by visualizing yourself as young and vibrant, you'll soon start to believe it. And when you believe it, you'll start behaving like it.

54

Relax and Enjoy
the Journey

∽

Growing old isn't a sentence; it's a celebration.

- People over the age of sixty-five get fewer illnesses than young people.
- Your brain can actually improve right into your nineties.
- A full one-third of people over sixty-five say they are living, or expect to live, the best years of their lives.

55

Help People

၄၀

A study of Chinese centenarians found that many were deeply involved in helping people (often for no money) and that they regarded helping their neighbors as a high daily priority.

56

Eat Less

∽

Experts say that eating less leads to less fat,
fewer poisons, and less stress on the digestive
system. So go easy on your food and live longer.

57

Enjoy a Regular Massage

❧

A good massage is a great antidote for stress. It can also help to reduce the buildup of lactic acid in the muscles, invigorate internal organs, and stimulate blood flow.

58

Become an Antiaging Expert

∾

Becoming an expert on longevity will change your life, literally.

There's a wealth of material in libraries, in bookshops, and on the Internet. And there's the biannual conference of the American Academy of Anti-Aging Medicine.

59

Stay Connected

෨

Studies show that people who interact with others may live longer than lonely people. The closer you are to others, the longer you'll probably live.

60

Sharpen Your Driving Skills

∽

Teen years aside, it's a statistically proven fact that your risk of auto accidents increases as you get older. So if you want to "drive to survive" when you're eighty, it's important to work on your skills (as well as your senses, muscles, and memory).

61

Work Yourself to Death

∽

Continuing to work long after the accepted
retirement age gives many people a sense of
fulfillment and self-worth. They're still independent
and making a contribution to society.

62

Try Ping-Pong

〰️

Ping-Pong, or table tennis, is a great fat burner. In fact, it's estimated that the exertion spent on Ping-Pong burns 355 calories an hour.

63

Avoid Food Additives

❧

Many people are allergic to food colorings and preservatives, such as monosodium glutamate (MSG), which is used in many Chinese restaurants. You can request that your meals be prepared without it.

To be on the safe side, whenever possible, eat fresh food.

64

Remember: Fresh Is Best

෧෮

Bacteria is an unwelcome and unrecognized additive in many foods. To avoid illness, make sure food preparation areas are clean, discard food in damaged wrappers, and check expiration dates.

65

Seek Out Fresh Air and Open Spaces

❧

Bansheng township in Guangxi, China, is renowned as a place where people live to one hundred and beyond.

It is situated in a mountainous region surrounded by woods and has a mild climate. There is no air or noise pollution, and people lead a quiet, secluded life.

66

Swim

❦

Swimming is one of the best forms of exercise
because it uses so many different muscles—so it
will help you get and maintain a good body
shape. It's also a terrific cardiovascular workout.

67

Eat an Apple (or Three) a Day

∾

The Chinese believe that eating three apples a day, one after each meal, can help reduce blood pressure.

68

Use Candles

∾

Candle power is less intense on the eyes than most electric lighting. Many people also feel candles are medicine for the soul.

69

It's Not Easy Being Green . . .

∽

Spinach and rhubarb contain oxalate, a chemical substance that interferes with the absorption of calcium.

If you're at risk of osteoporosis, eat both in moderation.

70

. . . But on the Other Hand

Spinach is one of nature's best tonics for
constipation. Mix a little spinach juice with carrot
juice, and flush away those blues.

71

Exercise Regularly,
Not Overly

∾

Shorter, more frequent bouts of exercise are better than occasional, longer sessions.

University of Nebraska specialists claim that three thirty-minute exercise routines burn twice as much fat as two forty-five-minute sessions.

72

Drink Green Tea

∽

Parts of Japan where green tea is drunk are said to have lower rates of cancer deaths.

73

Limit Sperm Loss

It may seem bizarre advice, but Chinese doctors claim that a good store of male semen massively boosts the body's immune system and energy levels. They say premature ejaculation causes premature aging.

74

Eat Your Carrots

∽

U.S. Department of Agriculture researchers claim that two carrots a day can reduce your cholesterol by as much as 20 percent.

75

Don't Smoke

∞

Numerous studies show that smokers are more likely than nonsmokers to die from heart disease—not to mention lung cancer.

76

Drink in Moderation

∾

A study of Californians found that people who consumed more than three alcoholic drinks a day had triple the risk of developing rectal cancer as nondrinkers.

77

Increase Oxygen
to Your Brain

∽

Lowering the fat and cholesterol in your diet and
increasing your intake of complex carbohydrates
can increase the oxygen in your brain—giving
you more energy and a clearer mind.

78

Get More Vitamin C

∾

Vitamin C is much more than a tonic for resisting colds. It's also known to play an important role in the prevention of cancer and the promotion of a healthy heart and vascular system.

79

Don't Stress

∞

Stress, anxiety, and the resulting depression can affect your natural immunity levels.

Studies have found that people who cope well with stress have better levels of natural-killer-cell activity (NKCA)—a measure of cellular immune function—than those who don't.

80

Seek a Harmonious Home

∾

The Chinese place great store on the importance of family harmony and mutual respect across the generations. They believe that a harmonious family environment can stave off dementia in the elderly.

81

Take Up Golf

෬

Notwithstanding your ability, golf is great recreation at any age—and it provides a great aerobic workout if you walk the whole course.

82

Develop a Green Thumb

∾

Gardening is great relaxation for the mind and exercise for the body.

Mowing the lawn, raking leaves, pruning, and planting give you a sense of accomplishment and a leisurely workout at the same time.

83

See a Dentist

❦

Visit the dentist twice a year. And remember that good old-fashioned brushing and flossing will help keep your teeth strong and your gums from receding.

84

Volunteer

∽

Become involved in your community. You'll get to
meet more people, develop new skills and
hidden talents, and broaden your perspective.

85

Eat Raw Foods
to Beat Fatigue

❧

A diet high in raw foods is a good tonic for
fatigue. Fresh green vegetables and sprouts are
high in both magnesium and potassium, while
raw fiber helps stabilize blood-sugar levels.

86

Jump Rope

❧

Regular physical exercise will help stimulate the
brain. Take up jumping rope, or walk up and
down the stairs a few times, or even do a few
simple stretches.

87

Don't Poison Your Brain

❦

To maintain a healthy brain, avoid undue
exposure to aluminum, zinc, other metals,
electromagnetic fields, industrial chemicals, and
pesticides.

88

Watch Your Blood Pressure

∽

Researchers in Sweden believe dementia may be
linked to high blood pressure.

89

Lift Weights

❧

Weight resistance training is a great way to boost your growth hormone levels. Just be sure you don't lift beyond your capacity.

90

Keep Up the Antioxidants

୶

Antioxidants—vitamins B, C, and beta carotene—
not only resist the effects of premature aging but
can also help heal sports injuries more quickly.

91

Don't Let Fat
Kill Your Sex Life

∾

Excess body fat can reduce sexual desire. That's because it upsets the balance of androgens to estrogens, which in turn undermines sexual desire, performance, and enjoyment.

92

Go Light on Meat

∾

Too much protein in your diet can lead to
calcium loss through your urine. That's because
protein binds with calcium in your digestive tract.

93

Don't Drive on the Weekends

∾

Statistics show that most fatal accidents occur on Friday, Saturday, and Sunday. So reduce your risk—stay off the road on those days.

94

Don't Share Smoke

∾

There's a growing body of evidence on the
detrimental effects of secondhand smoke. If
someone is smoking around you, leave the room.

95

Walk Off Your Stitches

∾

Walking is one of the best therapies for recovering from surgery (depending on the surgery, of course). It can improve both your physical and your emotional well-being.

96

Use Olive Oil

∞

Olive oil, together with avocados and nuts, is high in monounsaturated fat—the so-called good fat that can actually reduce cholesterol.

97

Stop Smoking . . .
It's Never Too Late

❦

Smokers can reduce their risk of heart disease
by 70 percent within a year or two of giving up
smoking, regardless of how long they've smoked.

98

Look for Lemongrass

∽

A University of Wisconsin, Madison, study found that lemongrass oil, used in Oriental cooking, reduced serum cholesterol by more than 10 percent in one-third of the participants.

99

Get a Mammogram

∾

Doctors say that women over the age of fifty should have a mammogram every year.

100

Wash Your Hands

∽

Old advice, but sound. And don't just rinse
quickly and shake—your hands may still contain
millions of bacteria.

101

Chew a Celery Stick

∾

Celery contains no fat, and it's a good source of vitamin A and potassium, as well as some calcium.

102

Slip, Slop, Slap

❧

Australia has one of the highest rates of skin cancer in the world—which is why Aussie health authorities recommend that you "slip on a shirt, slop on some sunscreen, and slap on a hat."

103

Exercise Your Eyes

❧

Like the rest of the body, eyes stay healthy longer when exercised. Each morning, roll your eyes several times in both directions, then practice looking at objects with your peripheral (side) vision.

104

Have Another Cup
of Green Tea

∾

Green tea contains polyphenols, which can lower
the "bad" and raise the "good" cholesterol, reduce
the risk of lung cancer among smokers, inhibit
blood platelet clotting that could cause a heart
attack, and help prevent UV damage to skin.

105

Use Vinegar and Baking Soda to Clean

൭

Good old-fashioned sodium bicarbonate (baking soda) and vinegar are two of the most effective, environmentally friendly, and safest all-around cleaners you can have in the home. You'll also save money.

106

Set an Age Target

❧

Select an age you'd like to live to. You're much more likely to change your lifestyle if you have a clear age goal.

107

Have Your Moles Checked

∽

Check your body for moles at least once a year, and keep a record of the size and shape of any you find. If you notice anything out of the ordinary (bleeding, itching, crusting, pain, etc.), see your doctor or a skin specialist.

108

Think About a
Water Purifier

∾

The U.S. Environmental Protection Agency
estimates that 58 million Americans drink tap
water that is contaminated in some way. A good
water filter may improve your water quality—
and your health.

109

Eat Potatoes

❧

They contain lots of potassium, which helps
reduce your blood pressure.

110

Trim That Gut

∾

Research in Sweden has found that people with potbellies have a higher risk of stroke than people who carry their fat on their bottoms, legs, or arms.

111

Go Easy on the Cheese

∽

A single slice of cheese can contain between 200 and 400 milligrams of sodium.

112

Get a Flu Shot

∾

If you're over the age of sixty-five, you should
have an annual flu shot before the influenza
season. You're at even greater risk from flu if you
have a history of chronic pulmonary or
cardiovascular disease.

113

Try Water First

❧

Hunger pains can be a sign that you're thirsty (which makes sense—food is up to 90 percent water). Drink a couple of glasses of water and wait ten minutes. You may not feel the need to eat as much.

114

Use a Hot Pack

⚬∾⚬

Studies have found that applying heat to a minor
wound helps increase blood flow and
oxygenation, which in turn can prevent infection.

115

Follow This Example

∾

What do the longest-lived populations in the world have in common?

They consume only one-half to two-thirds of the calories the average American does, a quarter of the fat, and half of the protein. Their carbohydrate intake is about the same, but is unprocessed instead of processed.

116

Save for Tomorrow

∾

It's important to have a savings plan that will support your lifestyle in your later years. Don't trust it to the government.

117

Have Another Serving
of Fruit

∾

One more helping of fresh fruit and vegetables a day could reduce your risk of a fatal stroke by as much as 40 percent, U.S. scientists believe.

118

Work, Work, and More Work

∽

A survey in *Centenarians* magazine found that 100 of the 555 persons surveyed were still making money after the age of one hundred.

119

Don't Bungee Jump

❧

Seventy percent of illnesses and deaths are
directly attributable to our behaviors—whether
that might be smoking, drinking, or skydiving.

120

Build a Relationship with Your Doctor

∽

Break down the traditional doctor-patient relationship. You're equal partners in your health, so don't be afraid to question or challenge your doctor. Learn to communicate with your doctor clearly and openly.

121

Be Resilient

∾

Accept the hand you've been dealt, whatever it is, and get on with your life. It's the only one you've got.

122

Heed the Experts

∽

Most medical and scientific experts agree on one thing: the three major killers in our society (cancer, coronary disease, and stroke) are linked to what we eat and drink.

123

Recharge Your Batteries

∾

Take time out to smell the flowers. Find a balance in your life between the demands of work, family, and play. You'll be happier, less stressed, and healthier in the long run.

124

Throw Away the
Remote Control

∽

The mere effort of getting up to change the TV
channel is a form of exercise, and over time it
will make a difference.

125

Maintain Your Balance

∾

Our bones get more brittle as we age, which means a relatively minor fall could cause a serious injury.

One way to combat this is to practice your balance. Try simple one-legged stands or, better still, practice Tai Chi.

126

Keep Moving

∾

One of the biggest causes of frailty in the aged is
inactivity. Once we slow down, our muscles start
to lose their strength at an estimated one
percent per day.

127

Have Your Prostate Checked

∽

Men: the U.S. National Cancer Institute recommends an annual prostate examination for men over the age of forty.

128

Start Your Meal
with Something Raw

∽

Heating food can destroy or render useless the enzymes in the food—and enzymes are important for good blood circulation.

129

Get Your Blood Flowing

∾

Reducing the fat in your diet will improve the
viscosity of your blood, enabling it to circulate
better and put less pressure on your heart.

130

Don't Dehydrate

❦

Dehydration doesn't just leave you feeling
thirsty—it robs your body of essential minerals,
such as potassium and sodium.

131

Don't Keep Birds

∽

You're more likely to develop lung cancer if you keep birds. It's thought that bird keepers inhale more allergens and dust particles than the rest of us.

132

See the World

∾

Travel broadens the mind. Embrace whatever you can to continually stimulate the mind and body, be it traveling to another country, visiting a museum, or taking in a gallery exhibition.

133

Don't Rush into a High-Fiber Diet

∿

You may experience some bloating, cramps, or gas buildup if you change your diet too quickly. Introduce extra fiber into your diet slowly—and at the same time increase your daily intake of water.

134

Find Out the Right Amount of Calories for You

୬୬

Your doctor should be able to give you a simple formula to calculate your ideal caloric intake. As a general rule, your daily intake should be no less than 1,200 calories if you're a woman or 1,500 calories if you're a man.

135

Drink Chilled Water

∾

In lowering body temperature, chilled water helps in a small way to use calories. The body has to work harder to make up for its heat loss by burning more fat.

136

Don't Overexercise

∾

Look for these warning signs, and if you have them, stop.

- Chest pains or palpitations
- Nausea or vomiting
- Extreme fatigue
- Shortness of breath
- Pain in the neck, jaw, muscles, or joints

137

Eat More Papaw
and Mango

∾

Both of these fruits are rich in an enzyme called
papain, which helps break down excess protein.
It's also good for cleaning the intestines and
helping relieve any digestive problems.

138

Beware: Heavy Drinking
Is Bad for Your Bones

❧

Australian doctors say that women who are
heavy drinkers are ten times more likely to
develop osteoporosis—and calcium supplements
won't help if they continue to drink.

139

Store Fruit and Vegetables Carefully

෨෯

Cover your salads with plastic wrap, even if
you're only ten minutes away from serving them.
It will help reduce oxidation.

140

Consume Fiber . . .
It's the Diabetic's Friend

∾

A high-fiber diet is good for diabetics. Soluble fiber can help slow food absorption and help keep the blood-sugar levels low.

141

Serve Up Salmon

∾

Eating as little as 5.5 grams of omega-3 fatty acids a month (the equivalent of four three-ounce servings of salmon) may reduce the risk of heart attack by up to half, according to University of Washington researchers.

142

Keep Up the Exercise

∾

A Harvard study of alumni has found that the
death rate from cancer is lowest among those
who exercise the most.

143

Eat a Grape or Three

∾

Grapes discourage the formation of mucus in the gut, so they're great for cleansing the liver, skin, intestines, and kidneys. They're also good for your blood cells.

144

Try Evening Primrose Oil

❧

Evening primrose oil can reduce cholesterol and
blood pressure. It has also been found to relieve
eczema and premenstrual tension, and is even
prescribed as a hangover cure.

145

Avoid Stress,
Avoid Disease

∾

A London hospital study found that fully half of one hundred women diagnosed with early-stage breast cancer had experienced a serious personal trauma (such as a bereavement or relationship breakup) in the previous year.

146

Buy Bagged Vegetables

∾

Researchers at the University of Kentucky have
found that supermarket vegetables that are pre-
bagged retain their vitamin C and beta-carotene
better than unwrapped vegetables because of
the controlled environment inside the bag.

147

Keep Smiling

∽

When you smile, your facial muscles activate the "feel good" chemicals in your brain.

148

Breathe Away
Your Headaches

∾

Taking a full, deep breath now and then can
reduce muscle tension and help prevent tension
headaches.

149

Retrain Your Memory

∾

Studies show that memory loss is reversible.
Asked to recall a random list of words, a group
of older study participants significantly improved
their recall after training and practice.

150

Choose Your Family

❧

Is longevity hereditary? According to a survey in China's Hubei Province, fifty-seven of eighty-eight centenarians have a history of long life in their families.

151

Keep Up the
Beta-Carotene

∽

Having three smaller intakes of beta-carotene a
day (found in dark yellow, orange, and dark
green vegetables) gives you three times the
benefit of taking it as one large dose.

152

Increase Your Calcium Intake

❧

There is more calcium in our bodies than any other mineral—yet in America, calcium (as well as iron) is deficient in most women's diets.

153

Avoid Shift Work

∾

When you work revolving shifts, your eating and sleeping patterns are disrupted and your body is placed under stress. It's believed that a person needs three to four weeks to resynchronize the body's circadian rhythms after working night shifts.

154

Urinate Regularly

∾

An Israeli study has drawn the conclusion that the more regularly you urinate, the less likely you are to suffer bladder cancer.

155

Dine Alone

∾

A Georgia State University study found that people consumed 44 percent more food when they ate with others than when they dined alone.

156

Consider Taking Estrogen

❧

Studies have found that women taking estrogen
have a greatly reduced risk of coronary disease
and stroke. Weigh that against a slightly higher
risk of breast cancer.

157

Choose Your Career Carefully

∾

Studies show that white-collar workers are more prone to cancer than their blue-collar colleagues.

158

Consider Taking Glutamine

∽

Glutamine has been shown in studies to help
reduce stress, build immunity, and rebuild the
body (and the muscles, in particular) after illness
or injury.

159

Be Wary of
Polyunsaturated Oil

❧

Examples include sunflower seed oil and sesame
oil. Although they lower "bad" (LDL) cholesterol,
they also lower the "good" (HDL) cholesterol.

160

Interact with Others

∾

Social interaction is important to your well-being—both physical and emotional—and hence a key strategy for living a long life.

161

Drink Your Juice

∾

Fresh fruit and vegetable juices are an excellent source of vitamins and minerals. That's because all the "goodies" are absorbed into the bloodstream as soon as they reach the stomach.

162

Get In Early

∾

Ninety percent of skin cancers are curable if detected early.

163

Start Your Meal Raw

❦

Try to start your meal with raw or lightly cooked foods, such as a salad or vegetables. They'll aid in the digestion of harder-to-digest foods, such as meat.

164

Try Frying with Olive Oil

∞

It contains only four fatty acids, so it's a healthier
alternative to frying with other oils. But
remember not to heat it to the smoking point.

165

Keep Up the Carbs

❧

The American Heart Association says that your daily intake of carbohydrates should represent 50 percent or more of your total calories. Sodium intake should be less than 2,400 milligrams a day.

166

Beat Stress

∽

Reducing the flow of cortisol (a stress-related hormone) reduces the wear and tear on your cells.

167

Listen to Classical Music

❧

Classical music (particularly Baroque style) has been proven to boost your learning ability.

168

Alternate Your Protein Sources

∽

Instead of meat, try to get your protein from nuts, beans, and broccoli.

169

Eat More Onions

∾

Harvard researchers who placed onion extract in a test tube containing cancer cells reported that the cancer cell growth greatly slowed.

170

Check Your Stools

∽

Colorectal cancer can be detected early if you give a stool sample to your doctor once a year.

171

Lower Your Exposure to Noise

❧

Japanese researchers believe that people regularly exposed to loud noise are twice as likely to have high blood pressure.

172

Let Your Seeds Sprout

༄

The benefits of eating seeds are multiplied many times when they are allowed to germinate (sprouts). The protein level rises, as does the vitamin content. Dormant enzymes also become active.

173

Get a Tetanus Booster

Everyone should have a tetanus shot every ten years—or every five if your work or leisure activities expose you to cuts or other wounds.

174

Choose to Be Happy

∞

Neuroimmunologists have discovered that happier people often have greater resistance to disease.

175

Chew Raw Food

∾

We need enzymes to trigger metabolism—and Nobel Prize winner Artturi Ilmari Virtanen says that chewing raw foods releases these all-important enzymes in the mouth.

176

Love Your Work

๛

More heart attacks happen at 9:00 A.M. on
Monday than at any other time. Choose your job
carefully.

177

Have a Regular Checkup

༄

You have your car checked regularly—why not
your body?

A thorough annual checkup—looking for any
early warning signs of serious ailments such as
heart disease, breast cancer, or prostate
cancer—is a must for everyone as they get
older.

178

Laugh a Lot

༛

Laughter increases the number of T cells, B cells, and immunoglobulins, all of which are important for your body's continued health.

179

Reduce Your
Red Meat Consumption

❦

It's often high in fat, and it's much harder to digest than fruit and vegetables, or even fish. The National Cancer Institute believes that diets high in red meat increase one's chances of developing cancer.

180

Take Your B Vitamins

❧

They're the stress busters and brain builders!

It's believed that the B vitamins—especially B_5 (pantothenic acid)—play an important role in relieving or reducing stress. Good sources of B_5 are egg yolks, fresh vegetables, whole wheat, yeast, kidney, and liver.

181

Develop a
Sense of Purpose

∽

According to world-renowned longevity expert
Dr. Vincent Giampapa people who have a sense
of purpose in their life tend to age more slowly.

182

Reduce Free Radicals

෨

Many experts believe that toxins known as free radicals are the number one cause of aging. To reduce them in your body, take vitamins C, B, and beta-carotene.

183

Don't Despair
Over Menopause

∽

Studies have found that women who approach
menopause with a positive attitude experience
fewer negative side effects.

184

Forget Frozen Vegetables

෪

Aging expert Dr. Ronald Klatz says that frozen vegetables have fewer vitamins than fresh. Dr. Klatz believes that most canned peas have lost over 90 percent of their vitamin C content.

185

Add Soybeans
to Your Diet

∽

The soybean is one of nature's great antiaging pills.

Dr. Denham Harman showed that laboratory animals that consumed soybean protein lived 13 percent longer.

186

Read Food Labels

෬

If sugar appears near the top of the list of ingredients, there's probably too much of it in the food you're buying.

187

Eat Raw Foods
to Fight Cancer

∽

Because of their alkalinity, raw foods help the
pancreas produce enzymes that fight cancer.

188

Eat Dandelion Leaves

❧

Great in salads, the young leaves of the
dandelion are a veritable treasure trove of
vitamins and minerals. They are particularly good
for arthritis sufferers because they are alkaline.

189

Try the Mediterranean Diet

∽

A diet rich in olive oil, whole-grain breads, and fresh fruit and vegetables increases one's life span, according to a report in the *British Medical Journal*.

190

Practice Fiber Power

❧

A high-fiber diet reduces your risk of colon cancer, varicose veins, and hemorrhoids. It's also great for the digestion.

191

Exercise . . . It Works

∾

Consider this: if you have high blood pressure
and exercise, you'll likely live longer than
someone with normal blood pressure who
doesn't exercise at all.

192

Put Broccoli
on Your Plate

∽

Broccoli is a fantastic source of fiber, a crucial
ingredient in any longevity diet.

193

Eat Red Fruits

ᕲᕴ

Tomatoes, strawberries, and watermelon, for example, contain lycopene and beta-carotene, both known cancer fighters.

194

Eat Your Greens

❧

Your mother was right.

Green lettuce, green beans, peas, and green cucumber are all excellent sources of minerals and vitamins.

195

Don't Get Angry

∞

Harvard Medical School showed that many heart attack victims had been angry only hours before their heart attack.

196

Avoid the Heat

∽

Researchers in Israel believe the risk of stroke is higher in hot weather. So if you're at risk, stay cool.

197

Enjoy Growing Older

❦

The good news is that more of us are living longer. It's estimated that there will be 140,000 centenarians in the world by 2004, and more than a million by the middle of this century.

198

Give Your Mind
a Workout

∾

We can train our brains to fitness, just like our bodies. Try to memorize long lists or names; play word-association games; and, most importantly, focus your concentration when you listen.

199

Aid Your Digestion

∾

Apart from tasting good, the herb dill is good for your digestion. It can also sweeten your breath, and is even claimed to be an aphrodisiac.

200

Watch Out for Ketchup

∽

Many brands of ketchup are very high in salt and contain numerous artificial colors and preservatives.

201

Reduce Fat in Your Diet

∾

Reducing the amount of fat in your diet and watching your cholesterol will reduce your risk of stroke and senility as you get older.

202

Eat Your Bean Soup

❧

Soups made with legumes (lentils, beans, and peas) are a great tonic and contain many trace elements that keep you healthy.

Their fiber content also helps to lower cholesterol and reduce the risk of colon cancer.

203

Drink Lots of Water

∾

Most people don't drink enough water. The U.S. National Research Council's recommended allowance for water is one and a half quarts per day.

204

Trust Your Doctor

∾

Despite the growth and popularity of alternative treatments, we still owe a lot to conventional medicine.

Thanks to advances in medical science, the death rate from heart disease has almost halved—and the fatality rate from strokes has more than halved—since the 1950s.

205

Try Kelp

∽

It's very nutritious and provides a balanced mineral intake. It's particularly high in iodine, which stimulates the thyroid to boost your metabolic rate, in turn burning off more fat.

206

Cook with Cranberries

∾

Cranberries and raspberries contain anthocyanin, which helps keep arteries from clogging by ensuring that our blood isn't too "sticky."

207

Add Color to Your Life

❧

Color therapy is great for health. Surround yourself with green or blue to calm your nerves. To increase your energy, wear yellow or orange.

208

Go Easy on the Coffee

∽

More than two cups a day wreaks havoc on your body's nervous system. There's also some evidence that coffee builds up serum cholesterol levels and increases the risk of heart trouble.

209

Give Your Brain a
Good Start to the Day

∾

A breakfast rich in complex carbohydrates and
high-quality protein can give your brain a charge,
improving the way you approach the day.

210

Don't Waste the Water

∞

If you must boil fresh vegetables, don't throw the water away. Cool it and drink it as a vitamin tonic.

211

Walk Off Those "T" Levels

∾

U.S. researchers believe that going for that evening walk may prevent the onset of prostate cancer. That's because exercise lowers testosterone levels. (High "T" levels are thought to be a link to prostate cancer.) But you need to walk at least ten miles a week—at any time of the day—for full benefits.

212

Get Involved

∽

Gerontologists believe that people who really engage in life usually live longer than others. So get out there and live. It's not just more fun, it's actually keeping you alive.

213

Take Shark Cartilage Tablets

༄

Cuban and Japanese research studies have found that shark cartilage can be a highly successful treatment for many types of cancer.

214

Become a Vegetarian

∽

The British Medical Association says that vegetarians live longer than meat eaters. Vegetarians have a 28 percent lower risk of dying from heart disease and a 39 percent reduced chance of dying from cancer.

215

Do Everything
in Moderation

❧

Much of what we hear and read about foods,
vitamins, minerals, and supplements seems to be
contradictory. Truth is, nearly everything we
consume has its upsides and downsides.

The best approach is to be informed, make
sensible judgments about your diet, and do
everything in moderation.

216

Take a Mineral Supplement

∾

Many diets are short on calcium, magnesium,
iron, zinc, and copper. A simple multivitamin once
a day can make all the difference.

217

Grow Your Own Sprouts

❧

Sprouts are a great health food, and they are easy to grow.

Use wheat, buckwheat, or sunflower seeds. Soak the seeds in water until they start to sprout. Sprinkle onto moist soil, cover the tray, and leave it for three days. On the fourth day, uncover your tray and continue watering (not too much) for about two weeks. Then harvest and enjoy.

218

Stay Active

∾

Find a balance between doing too little and too much—but most importantly, find something to do that makes you feel good.

219

Boost Your Fish Oils

∾

The oils from fish are called omega-3 fatty acids.
Women with a high concentration of omega-3
fatty acids in their breast tissues are five times
less likely to develop deadly tumors.

220

Avoid Alcohol for Healthy Bones

The Arthritis Foundation believes that heavy drinking puts both men and women at greater risk of bone fractures. Heavy drinkers have less bone mass and lose bone more rapidly than nondrinkers.

221

Watch Your Amino Acids

∾

Amino acids are the basic building blocks of the
40,000 different proteins in your body. See your
local health-food store for a good amino acid
supplement.

222

Keep Up Your DHEA

❦

DHEA levels are significantly lower in the elderly. Various studies have identified the importance of DHEA in keeping up your immunity level, reducing the risk of cancer and dementia, and fighting obesity.

223

Think Young

∾

A Harvard professor showed that old people who act like they are young may actually age at a slower speed.

224

Read Between the Lines

❦

Many manufacturers try to hide the actual sugar content of their products by breaking it down into terms like "dextrose" and "corn syrup"—so learn the terminology and don't be fooled.

225

Follow Supplement Guidelines

1. Always take vitamins with meals.
2. Always take amino acids on an empty stomach.
3. Spread out high dosages throughout the day.
4. To help digestion, drink lots of liquid when taking supplements.

226

Have a Selenium Drink

∾

Many cancer patients are short on selenium in their diets, according to Gerhard Schrauzer, Ph.D.

Mix it with your morning fruit juice to make a potent health drink.

227

Have Plenty of Garlic

∽

Don't worry about your breath: many garlic
tablets these days are odorless. Garlic promotes
energy, protects against free radicals, and reduces
stress hormones.

228

Drink Water, Water, and More Water

～

Remember, six to eight cups of water a day (in whatever form) is a good recipe for sound health.

229

Put Your Heart Problem
in Reverse

༄

Various studies have shown that the effects of
poor diet and lifestyle are reversible.

A low-fat diet coupled with exercise and
meditation can do wonders for your
cardiovascular system. It's never too late.

230

Take CoQ10

∾

It sounds like a scientific formula, but CoQ10 is in fact a potent nutrient for generating energy.

You can get CoQ10 from fish, grapeseed oil, many nuts, spinach, and soybeans, or in capsule form.

231

Take Ginseng,
the Ancient Wonder

❧

Ginseng has been a favorite of Korean, Japanese, and Chinese doctors for more than two thousand years. It's believed to have antitumor effects, as well as being an excellent general health tonic.

232

Take Vitamin C
for Brain Power

∽

Vitamin C really is the star of the vitamin world. In addition to everything else, it's a great brain food.

Other than supplements, some of the best sources of vitamin C are broccoli, brussels sprouts, cauliflower, strawberries, cabbage, oranges, lemons, and grapefruit.

233

Sleep

∾

Life is so busy, it's tempting to skip sleep. Don't. A shortage of sleep inhibits both the repair of your body and your mind's relaxation.

234

Get Up at the Same Time Daily

∽

The body needs order. Irregular sleep patterns increase bodily stress and can affect your ability to sleep. Try to go to sleep and wake up at about the same time each day.

235

Avoid Releasing
Those Free Radicals

∽

Studies have identified various sources that
induce free-radical chain reactions. These include
passive smoking, too much polyunsaturated fat in
the diet, air pollution, and X-rays.

236

Follow Deepak's Rules

∽

Dr. Deepak Chopra suggests six ways to increase longevity:

1. Respond creatively to change.
2. Reduce anxiety.
3. Focus on the ability to create and invent.
4. Maintain high levels of adaptability and flexibility.
5. Integrate new things and ideas into your life.
6. Want to stay alive.

237

Wear a Life Jacket

൭

It's estimated that 70 percent of fatalities on the
water arise from people not wearing life jackets.
If you're going boating, reduce your odds of
becoming a statistic by wearing a life jacket.

238

Walk with a Friend

∽

Involve others in your regular exercise routine. It
will encourage you to keep it going, and you can
give equal encouragement to your friend.

239

Get Rid of the
Loud Alarm Clock

❧

Some clocks frighten people into waking up. This, of course, can add up to a lot of extra stress over time.

Buy a radio alarm clock and tune it to a classical music station.

240

Protect Your Arteries

❧

Vitamin B$_6$ (pyridoxine) can help prevent artery damage that comes from consuming too much protein.

You'll find this vitamin in avocados, lentils, tuna, salmon, carrots, brown rice, bananas, soybeans, and wheat germ, among other foods.

241

Reduce Worry

∾

Worriers seldom live long lives; their nervous system packs up under constant stress. One way to reduce your worrying is to schedule it. Actually say to yourself that you'll do all your worrying from 3:00 to 3:30 P.M. Try it. It works.

242

Don't Diet

∾

Fat people tend to die younger than slim people,
yet diets often make you fatter in the long run.
It's much more effective to eat normally, but only
low-fat foods.

243

Always Eat Breakfast

∾

Some people think it's healthy to skip breakfast, but the opposite is true. A good breakfast not only fills you with energy, it also helps your mind process information faster and reduces bodily stress.

244

Associate with Young People

❧

The people around you have a huge impact on your quality of life and how long you live. Hang around with young people and you'll be much more likely to act and feel young.

245

Organize a
Support Group

∾

If you're suffering from a serious illness, getting
into a good support group is vital.

Dr. David Spiegel of Stanford University found
that cancer patients who participated in weekly
support-group sessions not only suffered less
pain and anxiety, but also lived twice as long.

246

Take Up Cycling

∞

Cycling gives your legs a great workout—and as
we get older, it's important to keep the leg
muscles in good condition.

247

Walk When You Can

∾

Try these tactics:

- Park your car a few blocks from work or home.
- Avoid the elevator.
- Always take the stairs.
- Don't eat at the nearest sandwich shop.
- Forget the car for short journeys.

248

Eat Choline-Rich Foods

❧

Foods containing choline help boost the brain's energy and memory functions. Try peanuts, wheat germ and whole wheat, eggs, white rice, lamb chops, ham, and calf's liver.

249

Get the Muesli Habit

∞

So many "health" breakfast cereals are packed
with sugar. Eating natural muesli is a far better
option. Muesli has the natural carbohydrates you
need for energy without going overboard on
sugar or artificial sweeteners.

250

Practice Qi Gong

〜

A very slow, gentle form of exercise, Qi Gong has been the subject of countless university research studies in China and has been found to have a powerful effect on the body's energy levels.

251

Don't Miss Out on Calcium

∾

The average male needs about 25 percent more calcium than he currently gets. You can get your calcium fix from low-fat dairy products, fish, fruits and vegetables, beans, grains, or, of course, calcium-supplement pills.

252

Don't Stress at the Gym

❧

People who push themselves to the limit when exercising are actually less healthy than those who take it easier in the gym or on the track.

253

Add Mushrooms
to Your Diet

∾

Shiitake mushrooms contain lentinal, a substance
that greatly boosts your T-cell production and
has been shown to help slow the spread of
cancer, particularly cancer of the lungs.

254

Exercise Away
Your Hunger

❦

A hunger attack can be staved off by a good,
brisk walk or other physical activity. Walking to
the fridge doesn't count.

255

Clean Your Home

∾

Long-term exposure to a dusty environment will affect your lungs and sinuses. A clean home helps create a healthy home.

256

Put the Zing Back with Zinc

❦

Zinc is great for male sexuality, as a shortage of zinc in men has been shown to contribute to a lower sex drive and lower sperm count.

Even arthritis may be helped by taking zinc.

257

Watch Out for Hot Dogs

∽

Those dogs could bite your insides to death.
Many hot dogs contain sodium nitrate, which
some cancer researchers believe can create
carcinogens.

258

Fast

∽

A one- or two-day fast not only gives your intestines a much-needed break but it also allows you to excrete toxins that may have been stored in your body for months.

259

Run Marathons

∾

In an amazing study, Dr. Tom Bassler carried out a worldwide analysis of mortality among marathon runners. His conclusion was that marathon athletes are virtually immune from heart disease, as long as they keep training.

260

Go Slow on Fast Foods

∽

Excess sodium is bad for you, and, unfortunately, most fast food is heavy on sodium. A Big Mac, for instance, has 890 milligrams of sodium— nearly 40 percent of the recommended daily allowance.

261

Don't Get Too Much Sun

∽

Your skin gets thinner as you get older, making it more susceptible to the sun's harmful rays. Skin-cell "turnover" also begins to slow down in your thirties, meaning that each layer of skin stays on your face longer.

262

Meditate

∾

Testing carried out since 1968 by such respected institutions as Harvard Medical School, Stanford University, and New England Hospital clearly shows that daily meditation can dramatically reduce stress and enhance physical and mental health.

263

Eat Grains, Grains,
and More Grains

໑໑

They are a proven source of fiber and can
reduce your risk of colon cancer. The more
unprocessed, the better. Go for whole wheat
flour, brown rice, cracked wheat, rye, oats, and
pasta.

264

Experience Tai Chi

෨

Tai Chi Chuan is one of Asia's great treasures. The slow, rhythmic movements of Tai Chi help unblock the body's energy rivers, known as meridians.

The result? Less stress, less disease, and, according to many believers, a longer life.

265

Get Married

❦

Statistically, couples tend to live longer than singles.

266

Eat Low-Fat Foods

೦೦

One in three Americans is clinically obese (20 percent above their ideal weight), and Australians are not much better. This is bad news, as there is overwhelming evidence that a high-fat diet increases the risks of cancer of the colon, breast, and prostate.

267

Buy Organic Fruit
and Vegetables

❧

It's a little more expensive, but it's usually much
cleaner, much purer, and more flavor-packed.

268

Get on the Juice

∾

A fruit- or vegetable-juice fast once or twice a year is a great idea—and if you're particularly keen, a one-day fast each week will do wonders.

Obviously, discontinue the fast should you feel sick, weak, or dizzy.

269

Don't Be Afraid

֍

Alzheimer's disease isn't as common as you think—in fact, it's estimated that only 10 percent of people over sixty-five have it, which means 90 percent don't.

270

Avoid Obesity to Reduce Breast Cancer Risk

∾

Some studies have associated obesity with a modest increase in the risk of developing breast cancer.

271

Keep Up the Zinc

୬୦

Tests on animals show that those short on zinc
are more prone to cancer.

272

Try Canned Tomatoes

∾

Lycopene, the cancer-fighting antioxidant found
in tomatoes, isn't destroyed by cooking or
canning. So if you can't get fresh, canned
tomatoes will do.

273

Unclog That Colon

∾

It's estimated that half the U.S. population has a clogged bowel—and poor diet is the biggest cause. (Putrefaction of matter in the colon can cause the release of toxins into the body.) A high-fiber diet is one of the answers.

274

Stay Away from Fat

∾

Up to 90 percent of the fat you eat comes back
to haunt you as body fat.

275

Take Comfort
in the Statistics

∾

Less than 5 percent of people over sixty-five in
the United States live in nursing homes. And the
great majority of those who live in the
community at large (95 percent) don't rely on
outside help in day-to-day activities.

276

Learn from the Japanese

∾

The Japanese have the longest life span in the world. They also have the highest daily intake of soybean protein.

277

Watch Your Weight . . . Not Too Light, Not Too Heavy

❧

Being underweight can be as bad for you as carrying too much weight. It's another reason not to get caught up in drastic fad diets.

278

Give Your Gut a Break

∾

It can take up to six hours to digest a high-fat meal, compared to two hours for a meal rich in carbohydrates.

279

Stay Off the White Bread

❦

It has usually had the fiber goodness processed
out of it and is loaded with sugar, salt, and fat.
Opt instead for whole-wheat, high-fiber, or
whole-grain breads.

280

Stay Active . . . You're
Never Too Old to Learn

∽

Make it a habit to learn something new every
week—whether it be a fact, a discipline, or a
new skill. An active mind equals an active body.

281

Don't Live in Russia

The average life span of Russians is still less than sixty. Gerontologists blame much of it on poor diet, high stress, and alcohol consumption.

282

Try Good Old Garlic

∽

The benefits of garlic go back a long time. It was used as a preventive treatment during the plague, and was packed in compresses to treat battlefield wounds during World War I.

283

Don't Smoke in Bed

∽

Fire statistics show that smoking just before
going to sleep leads to hundreds of deaths every
year in the United States.

284

Walk Off the Fat

∾

Your body uses about 100 calories to walk a mile. There are about 3,500 calories in a pound of fat. Do the math yourself: over time, a daily walk can make a difference.

285

Don't Forget:
Variety Is the Spice

∽

Don't focus on only a few foods. Your body can and should cope with many different foods—and a little of a lot is better than a lot of a little.

286

Try Lemon in Your Water

∽

Forget sugary cordials. A squeeze of lemon is a tasty and refreshing additive.

287

Remember This

∾

A Japanese study has found that people who walk have better memory retention.

288

Don't Eat Your Fiber
All at Once

⚭

It's much more beneficial to manage your daily fiber intake throughout the day—that way you'll avoid digestive problems.

289

Don't Overdo Painkillers

෧෨

Researchers believe that high doses of
nonsteroidal anti-inflammatory drugs—a popular
treatment for arthritis—may impair memory.

290

Nourish Your Brain

❧

Your brain requires at least 25 percent of the oxygen you breathe to function properly. Aerobic exercise is a great way to feed the brain and keep it in tip-top condition.

291

Take a Nap

∾

As you get older, you tend to sleep less. Try to compensate with a nap during the day. Again, it will boost your mental fitness.

292

Avoid Overtime

❦

A Boston University School of Medicine study has linked excessive overtime work to poor attention and decision making, not to mention tiredness and depression.

293

Practice Deep Breathing Daily

৩৩

Practice makes perfect. Pick a regular time to practice during the day and stick to it. Try first thing in the morning or before going to bed.

294

Avoid Anxiety Foods

❦

Certain foods can fuel anxiety. Avoid caffeine, alcohol, artificial flavorings, and sugar.

295

Don't Skip That Meal

It may just bring on a headache. Low blood-
sugar levels can trigger dilation of the blood
vessels in your head.

296

Be Sure You Really Need That Supplement

 ⌒⌒

Talk to your doctor or dietitian first—you may just need to change your diet.

297

Don't Drink Away
Your Immunity

∞

On top of everything else, alcohol is known to suppress your immune system, making you more susceptible to illness.

298

Check It Out . . .
Is Bottled Best?

∽

About 25 percent of bottled water is thought to
come from the same source as your tap water.
You may be paying a premium for something
that is no better (or worse) for you than what
you're drinking now.

299

Don't Let Disease
Slow You Down

❦

Chronic disease shouldn't stop you from exercising. Studies have shown that you can still derive benefits (improved cardiovascular response, muscle strength, and movement) from a good workout.

300

Lift Those Weights

༈

At Tufts University in Boston, a study of women
over the age of ninety found that all benefited
(in terms of strength and flexibility) from a
sustained weight-lifting program.

301

Prevent Prostate Cancer

∾

Researchers in the United States believe there is
a link between advanced prostate cancer and
the consumption of saturated fat, particularly
from red meat.

302

Get a Good Bed

୬୭

Sometimes we miss the obvious. A cure for
insomnia might be something as simple as a new
(and good-quality) bed.

303

Be Careful Mixing Drugs and Sex

∾

Many prescription drugs can interfere with sexual performance and desire. Ask your doctor before starting a medication.

304

Don't Be Treated
Like an Old Person

∽

Don't be patronized, brushed off, or spoken to rudely. Expect to be treated with respect—it's your right and you've earned it.

305

Set Goals

∾

Whether you're nineteen or ninety, know what
you want and plan how to get it. As we get
older, it's more important than ever that we fill
our lives with purpose.

306

Don't Waste Time

❦

People will tell you that you have more time on your hands as you get older—don't believe it. You have the same amount of hours and minutes in a day as everyone else, and you need to manage your time just as carefully and efficiently as the CEO of a major company.

307

Warm Up, Cool Down

૭૦

If you're going to do some strenuous exercise—whether it be a fast walk or a jog—it's important to warm up the "engine" beforehand and cool down afterward. Try some simple stretching before you start, and finish with some light walking.

308

Eat Foods with Boron—
It's Good for Brain Power

❧

Boron is found in fruits (apples, peaches, and
pears), legumes (beans, lentils), nuts, and leafy
vegetables, and has been found to aid learning
ability and mental alertness.

309

Juice Away Gout

∽

For relief from gout, try celery juice, parsley juice, or a mix of carrot, beet, and cucumber juice—and avoid fatty, salty foods and alcohol.

310

Chew Your Food

∾

Gandhi said to "drink your food and eat your
beverages." This is especially true of
carbohydrates, which rely on an enzyme in the
saliva for initial digestion.

311

Try Acupuncture

∾

There is growing evidence of the value of this ancient Chinese therapy for the treatment of all sorts of ailments, from muscle pain and headaches to cancer. It relies on stimulation of vital points on the body to manipulate the body's energy flow.

312

Make Exercise a Habit

∾

Get into a routine and try to stick to it. (That way you'll adjust both mind and body to a regime of exercise.) In the morning before breakfast is a good time for exercising—you can walk off yesterday's calories.

313

Try Eating the Apple Core

∽

True frugivores (fruit eaters) consume apple cores and seeds, the white fibers between orange sections, the seeds in grapes, and the like. These contain important enzymes and amino acids. But chew them to liquid first.

314

Eat for Beauty

❦

Vitamin C and bioflavin—found in many fruits and vegetables—help maintain the health of collagen, the fibrous protein that's behind good skin condition.

315

Make Your Raw Food Count

෨

Daniel Reid, in *The Tao of Health, Sex, and Longevity*, says that to get the most from a raw-food diet it must account for at least 50 percent of what you consume.

316

Follow the Chinese Diet

⁓

A survey of Chinese centenarians in the early
1980s found that beans and green vegetables
formed a major part of their diet. They relied
predominantly on carbohydrates for their calorie
intake.

317

Eat Wild Game

෩

Taoists have long believed that wild game, especially venison, is far better for us than meat from domestic livestock.

318

Eat Out Carefully

∾

You can still enjoy a wholesome, healthy meal straight off the menu at most restaurants—even some fast-food places. For example, go for pasta with just a tomato and basil sauce, or make salad your main course.

319

Take Calcium with Your Meal

෨

It's believed that calcium carbonate supplements are most effective when taken with meals. That's because stomach acids aid absorption of the calcium.

320

Don't Smoke
for Healthy Hips

∾

A U.S. study has found that women who smoke
have a 1.7 times greater risk of a hip fracture.

321

Accentuate the Positive

∾

As the old tune suggests, fill your vocabulary
(and your mind) with positive affirmations. It's
amazing what a difference it will make to your
whole outlook.

322

Spend More Time
with Your Kids

∽

Most of us are working harder and longer, and
losing quality family time. Think about what's truly
important in your life—and make changes, even
if it means sacrificing that pay increase or
promotion.

323

Prepare Your Kids Well

∾

Giving your kids challenging responsibilities around the home from an early age teaches them to solve problems and be more self-reliant—good training for their lives ahead.

324

Visualize Your Workout

෨

If it's hard getting started, do some mental prep
work: think about your exercise routine, how
good it will make you feel, and the long-term
benefits you will derive from it.

325

Take Your Medical History with You

೧෨

If you have a particular health condition or ailment, make a note of what it is, what you take for it, and who treats you, and carry it in your wallet. It's knowledge that just might help someone else save your life.

326

Practice Yoga

∾

Some of the healthiest people in the world are the yogis of India. Yoga maintains muscle tone in old age, and it's wonderful for both the nervous system and the brain.

327

Don't Drive with the Flu

∽

Researchers in Britain believe that a driver's
reaction time is impaired when the person is
affected by influenza. Even a bad cold can affect
hand-eye coordination.

328

Start Good Habits
at a Young Age

൬

U.S. researchers believe that girls can delay the
onset of ovulation by physical activity such as
swimming or running. And studies have found
that having fewer ovulation cycles lowers the risk
of breast cancer later in life.

329

Bank Your Blood

∾

Ask your local hospital or blood bank about building your own store of blood for an upcoming surgical procedure. It will reduce your risk of contracting any blood-borne viruses (such as HIV) from contaminated donor blood.

330

Wear a Skid Lid

∽

Whether on a bicycle or motorcycle, wear a helmet—it's a statistically proven lifesaver. And make sure it fits correctly.

331

Eat Your Prunes

∽

Not only are prunes high in fiber that can help prevent colon cancer, but they are rich in vitamin A, iron, and potassium.

332

Breathe Deeply

∞

Deep breathing not only energizes your body, it reduces stress—a crucial factor in preventing many diseases.

333

Beware of Headache

∽

A headache may be a precursor to a stroke. It's believed that a severe headache is a symptom in 99 percent of subarachnoid hemorrhagic strokes, as well as a common symptom of so-called mini-strokes.

334

Do Something About Snoring

❦

Snoring has been identified in numerous studies as a risk indicator or possible risk factor in high blood pressure, heart disease, and stroke.

335

Go Easy on the
Soy Sauce

∽

It might taste great in your oriental cooking, but it's packed with sodium. Use low-salt soy sauce, and sparingly at that.

336

Monitor Your Blood Pressure

๛

Keep a chart so you can track your blood pressure. And check your blood pressure at work (when you're likely to be under more pressure).

337

Grow a Philodendron or Two

∾

One of the best indoor plants for filtering out carbon monoxide and other airborne nasties is the philodendron.

338

Be Careful About Whom You Sleep With

∾

The risk of contracting AIDS from unprotected, casual sex is highest with partners who are homosexual or bisexual men, intravenous drug users, hemophiliacs, female prostitutes, or heterosexuals from high-risk areas like central Africa.

339

Avoid Artificial Tanning

∾

The U.S. Food and Drug Administration says that ultraviolet A light (used in some tanning booths) can increase your risk of skin cancer. Ultraviolet B can also cause skin cancer.

340

Have an
Orange Juice Chaser

∿

After eating nitrate-rich foods, follow up with
orange juice. Nitrates are used to preserve some
meats (such as bacon and bologna) and have
been linked to cancer-causing nitrosamines.
Orange juice is believed to act against
nitrosamines.

341

Walk in Water

❧

As an alternative to jogging or walking on land,
try walking in the pool for twenty minutes, three
times a week. It's a great calorie burner—and it's
low impact, which means there's little risk of
injury.

342

Try Fry-Free Fries

∾

As a healthier alternative to traditional fries, cut up your own potatoes, spray with a nonstick cooking oil, and place in the oven on a nonstick tray. Bake for fifteen to twenty minutes at 450 degrees, turning once.

343

Take Up Tennis

❦

You're never too old to throw down an ace. You might not hit the ball as hard, but you can compensate in other ways. For example, use a two-handed instead of one-handed backhand, or try to slice the ball so it's harder to hit back.

344

Eat More Oats and Barley

∾

Both have been found to do wonders in helping
fight high cholesterol.

345

Exercise Off Diabetes

∞

U.S. medical researchers believe that the risk of developing the most common form of diabetes—adult-onset diabetes—can be significantly reduced by exercise.

346

Rehydrate After Exercise

∽

For hard exercise that lasts more than ninety minutes, some nutritionists recommend rehydrating with a sports drink. But or most people, a couple of glasses of good, old-fashioned water will be sufficient.

347

Say "Low-Fat Cheese, Please"

∽

Although it's great for calcium, cheese is also loaded with saturated fat. Go for the low-fat, low-salt varieties.

348

Have Your Eyes Checked

∾

As you grow older, your vision may become impaired, increasing your risk of falls and bumps. Regular eye tests will also pick up any indications of glaucoma.

349

Eat Brown Rice, Not White

∽

White (processed) rice has much of the fiber goodness taken out of it. And experts believe that eating too much starchy, fiber-depleted food may increase your risk of diabetes.

350

Give Your Liver a Break

∽

If you drink every day, try to build two or three alcohol-free days a week into your regime. Your liver will thank you.

351

Keep Fit and
Breathe Easier

∽

Your body's oxygen-carrying capacity decreases
significantly faster with age if you are unfit—so
keep your body in shape, and you'll be breathing
easy until you're one huundred.

352

Have Some Yogurt

∾

But make it the low-fat variety. Yogurt is rich in calcium and potassium to help fight osteoporosis, stroke, and high blood pressure.

353

Get a Good Pair of Shoes

∞

Ill-fitting shoes will create a mental and physical pain barrier that may stop you from exercising. It's important to be comfortable when you walk or jog—and shoes are the most important source of comfort.

354

Skip the Soft Drink

∾

A regular can of soda pop contains the
equivalent of about nine teaspoons of sugar.

355

Say You're Sorry
and Forgive Others

∽

Don't hold in guilt or resentment. It will just
contribute to your anger and stress levels.

356

Have Your Cholesterol Checked

❧

High cholesterol increases your risk of heart attack. See your doctor to have it checked (it involves a simple blood test). You can then adjust your diet and lifestyle accordingly.

357

Walk the Dog

∾

Yet another incentive to get you moving—and you'll both enjoy it.

358

Quit Your Job

∞

If it's causing you too much stress or contributing to an unhealthy lifestyle, have the courage to walk away and find something better. But first determine the real cause of your problems: it might be more deep-seated than your job.

359

Surround Yourself
with Plants

∾

Plants do more than pump out fresh oxygen all
day long; they also bring a feeling of calmness to
people living around them.

360

Try Cooking Without Salt

∽

Salt is only there to add flavor, and flavor is totally subjective. You'll soon get used to a salt-free taste. And while you're at it, skip the sugar in your coffee. Once you're used to it, you'll never go back.

361

Use Unbleached Filters

~

Use unbleached filters for your drip coffeemaker.
Bleached filters contain dioxin.

362

Trim the Fat

✺

Trim your meat of fat before (and after) cooking.
And try chicken without the skin as a healthier
alternative.

363

Fire the Maid

∾

Housework can be a great all-over workout. Your body will appreciate the exercise, and your outlook will benefit from the sense of achievement.

364

Go Window Shopping

෨

Whatever distraction it takes to get you walking!
A few laps at the mall will do wonders for your
fitness—just leave the credit card at home.

365

Go Natural

Take a walk in the park, sit on a beach or by a river or atop a mountain ... the natural world can have a wonderful, calming effect on your outlook. Take it in.

Other Longevity Titles

∞

Stopping the Clock, by Ronald Klatz and Robert Goldman

Dare to Be 100, by Walter M. Bortz II, M.D.

Feel 30 for the Next 50 Years, by David W. Johnson, Ph.D.

Look Ten Years Younger, Live Ten Years Longer, by David Ryback

Quantum Longevity, by Vincent Giampapa (available from Longevity Institute International in New Jersey)

Lifespan Plus, by the Editors of *Prevention* magazine

Earl Mindell's Vitamin Bible

Live Long, Die Fast, by John H. Bland, M.D.

Brain Fitness, by Bob Goldman with Ronald Klatz and Lisa Berger

Time of Our Lives, by Tom Kirkwood